AF480069

GOOD MORNING, *Love!*

Beginning Each Day with God's Word & Positive Thoughts

Leta Coleman

Grace Impact Publishing, LLC. New Orleans, LA.
Published by: Grace Impact Publishing, LLC New Orleans,
LA
www.GIPublishing.com
Info@GIPublishing.com

ISBN: 979-8-218-05908-8

Good Morning, Love! Volume 1 / Leta Coleman
Self Help/Motivational and Inspirational
Self Help/Spiritual
Self Help/Personal Growth

Leta Coleman
Los Angeles, CA
Website: www.LetaColeman.com

Published in New Orleans, LA
Printed in the United States of America

Table of Contents

I Dedicate this Journal

to my mother, Ruth.

Your Prayers and Faith

reset my path, with Purpose.

Introduction

"My voice You shall hear in the morning, O Lord; In the morning I will direct it to You, And I will look up." Psalms5:3

Have you ever felt like you've just laid your body down to rest and as quickly as your eyes close, it's time for them to open again? Depending on how we shape our thoughts around a new day, our "eyes opening" can feel great and refreshing or like you just want to hit the snooze button.

When we set time to shape our thoughts each morning using the Word of God and intentional positive thoughts, we ensure that we enter each day feeling like we've already won!

"Good Morning, Love!" was written from a place of heartfelt love in hopes that you will jump start each morning with gratitude, excitement, and new joy to take on the day! It can be difficult to always feel the goodness of the morning when those sleepy eyes part their way.

Allow "Good Morning, Love!" to be a Divine tool to break forth into a new day with God, His Word and your reminder of why THIS DAY is so very special.

This work began in Pacific time (California to be exact) as a morning text message of inspiration all across the country. God has exceeded the expectation and graced this work be a beautiful, tangible piece of inspiration and art to greet you a beautiful: "Good morning, Love!"

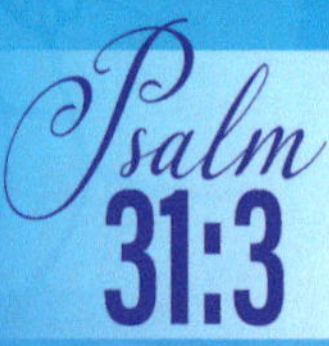

Good Morning, Love!

We can ask and trust that

God's lead

is the Best way, for He has a plan for us that far exceeds our imagination and expectations and it will not fail. Seek him for guidance daily.

My Prayer for Today

____

____

____

____

____

____

____

WE HAVE THIS
Hope
AS AN
ANCHOR
for the
SOUL,
FIRM & SECURE.
HEBREWS 6:19

Give careful thought to the paths for your feet and be steadfast in all your ways. Amen

Good Morning, Love!

To Seek

God's Will

for all areas of your journey is an assurance that your Trust in Him will bring forth a Perfect Plan.

My Prayer for Today

When I thought,
"My foot slips,"

YOUR STEADFAST *love* O LORD, held me up.

PSALM 94:18

Romans 15:13

May the God of hope fill you with all joy and peace as you trust in him, so that you may overflow with hope by the power of the Holy Spirit. Amen

Good Morning, Love!

Never give up

HOPE

Hope for a bright Future, Hope for your hearts desires, Hope for Dreams and visions that bring fulfilment in

Life & Love.

My Prayer for Today

____

____

____

____

____

____

____

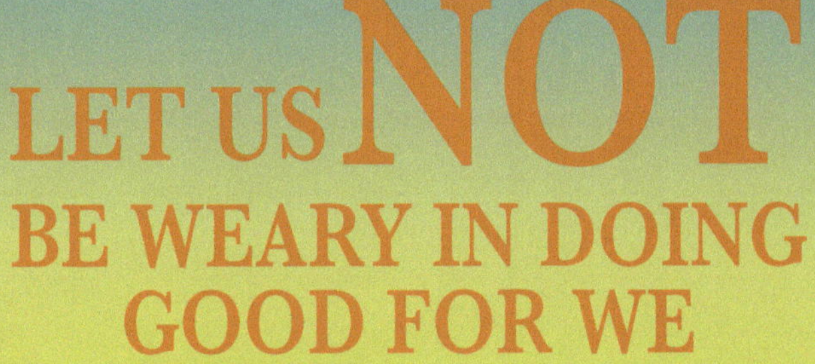

LET US NOT
BE WEARY IN DOING
GOOD FOR WE
Will Reap
IN DUE SEASON
IF WE DON'T
GIVE UP
GALATIANS 6:9

Good Morning, Love!

Faith & Hope

brings things into fruition. Let's activate the vision and promises He has shown us in His word.

My Prayer for Today

SHOW
GOD
YOUR
Faith
AND HE WILL
SHOW YOU HIS
Faith-fulness

Let your eyes look straight ahead; fix your gaze directly before you. Amen

Good Morning, Love!

Let's focus on what
is ahead for us with

Faith that
ALL THINGS

are working out for our Good...

Favor is on the horizon!

My Prayer for Today

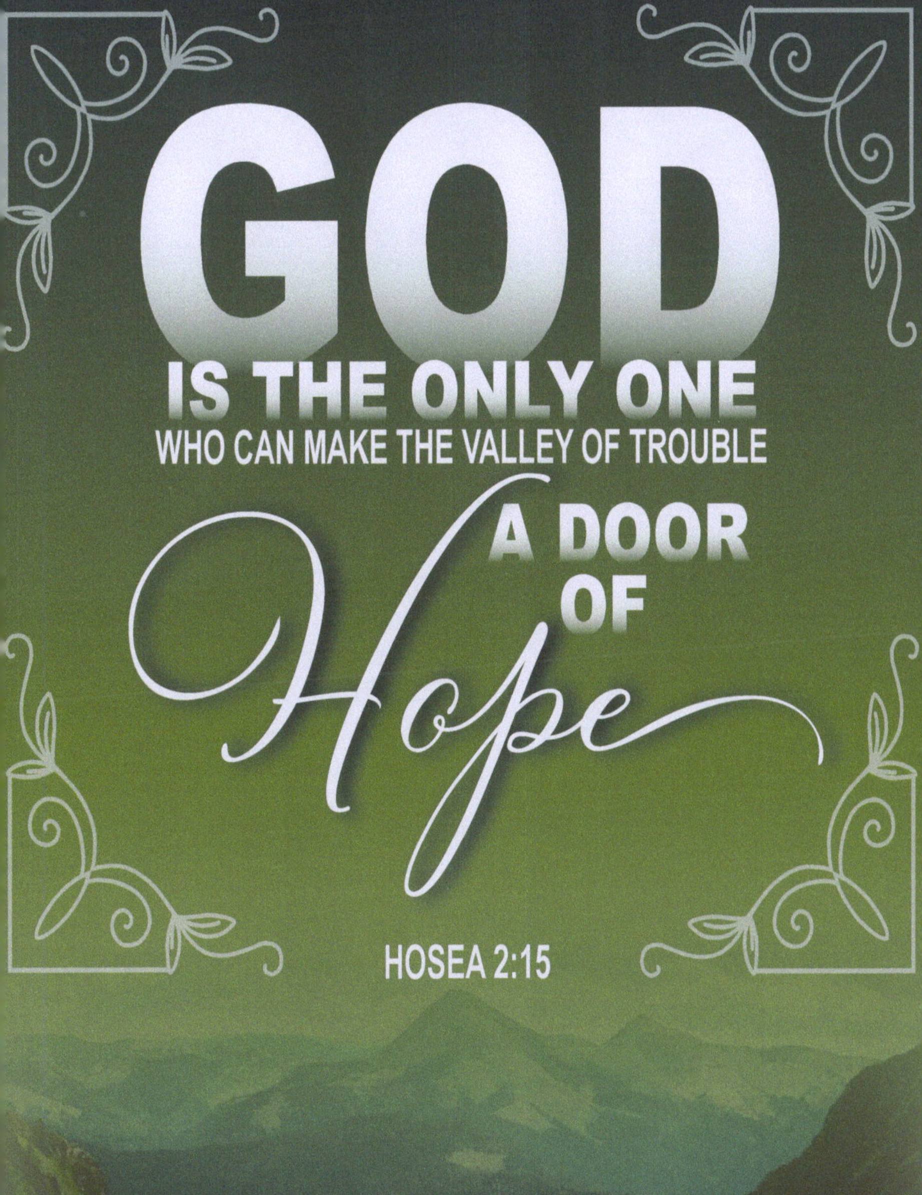
GOD
IS THE ONLY ONE
WHO CAN MAKE THE VALLEY OF TROUBLE
A DOOR
OF
Hope
HOSEA 2:15

Good Morning, Love!

My Prayer for Today

____
____
____
____
____
____
____

God
WILL MEET
ALL YOUR
needs.
PHILIPPIANS 4:9

Good Morning, Love!

Let your heart not be troubled. Let your request be known and know that He will take care of you.

Stay focused on Him!

My Prayer for Today

I HEARD YOUR PRAYER. TRUST MY TIMING.

—God

The Lord on high is mightier Than the noise of many waters, Than the mighty waves of the sea. Amen

Good Morning, Love!

We must remember God's word is

Yes & Amen

His thoughts towards you says the Lord, thoughts of peace and not of evil, to give you a future and a hope.

My Prayer for Today

God's
Word is
Yes
&
Amen

Good Morning, Love!

Remember

His Plan

is to prosper us, not to cause us harm.

My Prayer for Today

Give Thanks
to the LORD
FOR HE IS GOOD! HIS
FAITHFUL LOVE
ENDURES FOREVER.
Psalm 136:1

Philippians 4:8 | Finally, brothers and sisters, whatever is true, whatever is noble, whatever is right, whatever is pure, whatever is lovely, whatever is admirable—if anything is excellent or praiseworthy—think about such things. Amen

Good Morning, Love!

To remain in a mindset of

Peace

set your heart and thoughts
on that which is Good.

My Prayer for Today

____

____

____

____

____

____

____

DON'T LET ANYTHING STEAL YOUR JOY!

Good Morning, Love!

When the winds are blowing and Peace is not easily obtainable. Those thoughts of doubt, confusion, unsettling objections to the will of God. Remember be anxious for nothing, don't move or respond out of fear or confusion Speak to the winds with Authority...

Peace, Peace, Peace in the name of Jesus.

My Prayer for Today

____

____

____

____

____

____

____

God
SUPPLIES
PEACE
& JOY
when you believe!

Be careful for nothing; but in every thing by prayer and supplication with thanksgiving let your requests be made known unto God. Amen

Good Morning, Love!

Remember, God is all knowing and it's not by mistake that these things have come against you. But He promised us, He will protect us and keep us from falling. Remember the plan...

My Prayer for Today

WE CAN MAKE OUR PLANS BUT THE LORD DETERMINES OUR STEPS.

Good Morning, Love!

As we have

Hopes & Dreams

when we seek God's guidance,
we will see Favor

My Prayer for Today

____
____
____
____
____
____
____

SOMETIMES GOD DOESN'T CHANGE YOUR SITUATION BECAUSE HE IS TRYING TO CHANGE YOUR HEART.

James 1:4 | But let patience have its perfect work, that you may be perfect and complete, lacking nothing. Amen

Good Morning, Love!

WHEN WE EXERCISE
PATIENCE
THE RESULTS ARE PROFITABLE.

My Prayer for Today

____

____

____

____

____

____

____

What is
FOR YOU, WILL NOT
PASS YOU.

My Prayer for Today

GOOD THINGS COME TO THOSE WHO *Believe,*

BETTER THINGS COME TO THOSE WHO ARE *Patient*

THE BEST THINGS COME TO THOSE WHO *Don't Give Up!*

Good Morning, Love!

DAILY REMINDER:

When Praises go up, blessings come down. The gift of Peace, Good Health, Contentment, Prosperity and just knowing you have no need to worry for He will take care of you. Remember to Praise Him all throughout your day.

My Prayer for Today

IT'S NOT LUCK, IT'S GOD'S Favor

From the fullness of His grace we have all received one blessing after another. – John 1:16

Good Morning, Love!

Because we have value and purpose, may God's mercy and grace sustain you.

Remember His Grace

is our strength

My Prayer for Today

Commit your work to the
Lord,
AND YOUR
PLANS
will be established.
Proverbs 16:3

The Lord shall fight for you, and ye shall hold your peace. Amen

Good Morning, Love!

Remember, He created us to worship Him. He wants us not to worry. He will hide you. He will bring you no harm. He protects you. Trust and follow His lead ...your silent Partner.

My Prayer for Today

GOD MADE YOU A
Masterpiece

START SEEING YOURSELF STRONG,
HEALTHY, ACCOMPLISHING
YOUR DREAMS AND LIVING HIS
ABUNDANT LIFE.

Good Morning, Love!

Those visions of creativity of prosperity, business success, are the blueprints to your future take note

My Prayer for Today

____

____

____

____

____

____

____

For God has NOT given us a spirit of
Fear
but of POWER & of LOVE & of a SOUND MIND.
2 Timothy 1:7

Good Morning, Love!

Remember, His burdens are light; take it to Him in **prayer.**

My Prayer for Today

Wisdom

will multiply your days and add years to your life.

Proverbs 9:11

Good Morning, Love!

Do your best to stand and walk
with Love, Wisdom and Integrity,
not to bow down to that which
God has placed under your feet.

Rise up ...

My Prayer for Today

____
____
____
____
____
____
____

THOSE
WHO SEEK THE
LORD
SHALL NOT
LACK ANY GOOD THING.
Psalm 34:10

Romans 11:29 for God's gifts and his call are irrevocable.

Psalm 23:1 A psalm of David. The Lord is my shepherd; I have all that I need. Amen

Good Morning, Love!

Be still and know that God will provide and He hears your request...

My Prayer for Today

HE WILL
SUSTAIN
YOU.
Isaiah 46:4

Psalm 31:3 Since you are my rock and my fortress, for the sake of your name lead and guide me. Amen

Good Morning, Love!

We can ask and trust that God's lead is the Best way for He has a plan for us and it will not fail. Seek him for guidance daily.

My Prayer for Today

Be strong and courageous
do not be frightened do not
be dismayed for the Lord
your God is with you

Joshua 1:9

Our Father in heaven, Hallowed be Your name. 10 Your kingdom come. Your will be done on earth as it is in heaven. 11 Give us this day our daily bread. 12 And forgive us our debts, as we forgive our debtors. 13 And do not lead us into temptation but deliver us from the evil one. For Yours is the kingdom and the power and the glory forever. Amen.

Good Morning, Love!

Our daily Prayer is our communication line to our creator. We speak our desires in Hope they will be granted to us. My prayer for you is that God will always make himself known to you and He will continue to cover and keep you in His Promises.

My Prayer for Today

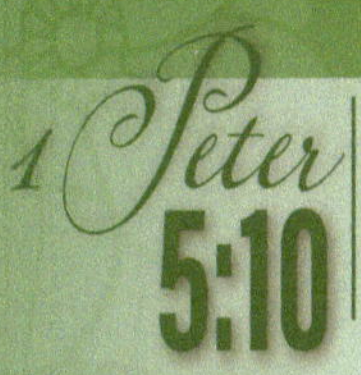

And the God of all grace, who called you to his eternal glory in Christ, after you have suffered a little while, will himself restore you and make you strong, firm and steadfast. Amen

Good Morning, Love!

No matter the situation or challenge. Call on the name of the Lord. His name is your source of Power.

My Prayer for Today

Journal

Journal

Journal

Journal

Journal

Journal

Journal

Journal

Journal

Journal

Journal